"OMG ~ I'm Praise Dancing! Now What?"

A Guide Encouraging You to 'Go Ahead' and Dance!

By Stephanie Esters

Purposed Publishing 8:18

Purposed Publishing 81:8 publications and other items are available at www.purposedpublishing818.com.

OMG ~ I'M PRAISE DANCING! NOW WHAT? (A Guide Encouraging You to 'Go Ahead' and Dance!) By Stephanie Esters
Published by Purposed Publishing 8:18
www.purposedpublishing818.com

All rights reserved. No part of this book may be reproduced or transmitted in any format (print, digital/electronic or other) or medium or stored on any data retrieval system or device without the written permission of the author.

Scripture from The NIV Student Bible, Revised (Zondervan), unless otherwise noted.

Copyright © 2015 by Stephanie Esters
All rights reserved

First edition 2015

Library of Congress Cataloguing-in-Publication Data
    Esters, Stephanie
    Omg ~ I'm Praise Dancing! Now What? / Stephanie Esters

ISBN: 978-0-9838097-4-6

Library of Congress Control Number: 2015936930

By Stephanie Esters
Purposed Publishing 8:18

Printed in the United States of America

*In memory of
the wind beneath my wings ...*

Daddy and Momma

~ Table of Contents ~

Dedication .... *iii*

Foreword .... *vii*

Preface .... *ix*

1. OMG, I'm Praise Dancing 1
2. 'Cause God Said So! 3
3. Work It Out! 5
4. Consecrate In the Shadows 8
5. Just Flow 10
6. Just One More Time 12
7. Listen to What God Says 14
8. No Grief, Please! 17
9. Pull Your Clothes Together 19
10. Self-Critique, Please! 23
11. Know That You Are and Have A Gift 25
12. Now What? 27
13. Notes Page 30
14. Resources 31

    Bibliography 34

    Index 37

FOREWORD

The title of this book reflects that thought that some of us might suddenly find ourselves entertaining: *"OMG ~ I'm praise dancing! Now what?"* ☺ We may go on to question, 'But how do I know God chose me for this?' or 'Why would God want to use <u>me</u> in this ministry; I'm not a dancer? I don't even know anything about praise dance!'

Well you can now rest assured! This book walks us through some of the questions that we, as praise dancers, may have asked ourselves at one time or another, the kind of thoughts we may have even been too embarrassed to ask out loud. *How do I worship God in dance? Why is it important to have my own garments? Can we dance if we've never had any experience?* And here's one of <u>the</u> most critical (my favorite) questions: *What's the big deal about undergarments --- why are they important?*

"OMG ~ I'm Praise Dancing! Now What?" shares God's truth on these tough questions, not only for the new dancer, but for the seasoned dancer as well. I believe that everyone --- corporate dance ministries as well as the individual liturgical minister --- can benefit from this amazing teaching

While reading *"OMG ~ I'm Praise Dancing! Now What?,"* I experienced God's call to excellency in my personal dance ministry to Him. There were times I even got chills reading about the beautiful worship experiences that Stephanie has had during her private dance ministry unto God! *(I also love the fact that I sat in Barnes and Noble and read a draft of this book in less than an hour . . . it's an easy read!)*

Our character is flawed, yet God's is perfect! Is He sure He wants to use me? The answer is a resounding *'yes'!*

Biblical, real, funny and inspirational, *"OMG"* encourages us that, no matter where we are in our dance-ministry journey, *we are called to dance!* Self-doubt always has a way of trying to enter, but prepare to be reminded of who you are in God's eyes; to be comforted; to be strengthened and to be encouraged as you fall into the arms of the Great I Am. He is speaking life through this book and gives us more than enough reassurance that He wants us to go forth and dance!

Thank you, Stephanie, for taking on what I believe are leading subjects and questions that dance ministries face and for doing this with sound Biblical teaching. For more than eight years now, I have witnessed you grow into being such a huge blessing in the dance ministry world, as well as outside of this circle! You are such an inspiring, faith-filled servant of God and wonderful sister-friend to me and others! *I'm so grateful that the world gets to finally partake of the gifts that God has poured into you!*

Jasmine Robinson, Visionary
Leaps of Faith Dance Company

PREFACE

While preparing to meet with a small group to help start its adult praise- dance ministry, I reviewed a few key points I wanted to share with them about how I taught praise dance and what I wanted them to learn. This small guide ~ *"OMG ~ I'm Praise Dancing! Now What?"* ~ grew from some of my notes out of that meeting. It is a primer to help first-time praise-dance ministers slay any apprehension they have and move resolutely and decisively into ministry --- *in excellence.*

This small book is a *"why-and-how-I-do-what I-do."* *"OMG ~ I'm Praise Dancing! Now What?"* boils down more than 15 years of Biblical dance study and eight years of public praise dance ministering and teaching into a format that is easily digestible for the 'newbies' to this ministry. This guide covers some areas that I had to master to move toward excellence --- things I had to learn on my own, but that I wished I'd had someone telling me early on in my ministry. I urge you to immediately obey the Holy Spirit and move intentionally and boldly into the dance ministry, so you can start to make a difference for and in the Kingdom. I allowed almost eight years to lapse before I answered the call to move into dance ministry, paralyzed by self-doubt and fear (2 Timothy 1:7), which, of course, we know is not from Our Father! Additionally, this guide attempts to answer questions that those newer dancers and others have asked me, while providing encouragement to continue growing in their personal walk with God and in their dance ministry.

"OMG ~ I'm Praise Dancing! Now What?" is divided into 12 neat little chapters that discuss:

- Why Bible study and prayer and spending time in God's presence are as important as the 'garments' --- those gloriously beautiful clothes --- that need to be part of your ministry arsenal;
- Why practice and more practice really do make perfect-*ed*;
- How praise dance is ideal for street evangelism --- reaching those outside the walls of the church, among other topics.

It is my goal that you learn that you need to move quickly and masterfully into the praise-dance ministry. I pray that this guide blesses your ministry and keeps pointing you in the direction of **Our Master Dance Teacher!**

Stephanie Esters
21 March 2015

"OMG ~ I'm Praise Dancing... Now What?"

~ Chapter 1 ~

Are you thinking *"Oh, my goodness --- I'm praise dancing! How did this happen? Now what?"*

If you find yourself thinking this, know that you are not the first or only one to have experienced these thoughts! I am trusting that you believe God directed you to this area as ministry. On that note, *"Congratulations!"* Bless you for making that leap that God directed you to make for His Kingdom! He wants to use you, so please stay open and available to Him!

Know that He called you and ordained you for such a time as this *"because of his own purpose"* (2 Timothy 1:9)! Prepare to enjoy this experience, endeavor to remain useful for God and remember to keep growing! I sum this up with the words I heard as I returned from a Dancing Preachers conference a few years ago: *"Run with the head of the pack."* To me, this meant staying hungry for The Word and how God wanted to move me in this ministry. It also meant soaking up what Godly people poured into me, then pouring out onto others the knowledge and experience I had. That 'iron sharpens iron' scripture comes to mind (Proverbs 27:17).

So if you're called to dance, you *gotta* dance! It does not matter that you've never taken a dance class before or that you, quote-unquote, "can't dance." Many people have told me, "but I can't dance," and I tell them that God's Word says He is seeking those who have a heart of worship for Him (John 4:23-24).

If called, you must come forth! It could mean life and death for someone else!

> "For if you remain silent at this time, relief and deliverance for the Jews will arise from another place, but you and your father's family will perish.
> "And who knows but that you have come to the royal position for such a time as this?"
>
> ~ Esther 4:14-15 (Student Bible, NIV)

Decide to move forward in the ministry of dance with holy confidence (Galatians 2:20); with a lion-like boldness (Proverbs 28:1); and with a decisive resolution (Romans 12:11) to minister your job well! *Watch God meet you there!*

POWER POINTS
- *Stay 'useful' for God*
- *Stay 'hungry' ~ "Run with the head of the pack!*
- *'Dance' like someone's life depended on it!*

'Dance like someone's life depends on it!'

" 'Cause God Said So!"

~ Chapter 2 ~

There were quite a few times in my ministry when I second-guessed myself: *Why am I dancing in the church? What is this all about? What is this thing called 'praise-dancing'?*

I learned, from God's Word, that I'm not the first one inspired to dance before and for God. Take a look at these instances of dancing cited in the Bible --- most for good, one for not:

- **Celebrate:** Exodus 15:20, 1 Chronicles 15:29, Psalm 30:11a, Psalm 150:4
- **Prophesy:** 1 Samuel 18:6-7
- **Encourage**: Psalm 30:11
- **Draw away / destroy / kill**: Mark 6:14-29, Matthew 11:1-17 (*We definitely do not want to be accused of this kind of dancing that led to such drastic --- and fatal --- consequences!*)

Know that Word calls us to *praise Him* in the dance:

"Praise Him with the sounding of the trumpet,
praise Him with the harp and lyre.
"Praise Him with tambourine and dancing,
"Praise Him with the strings and flute
"Praise him with the clash of the cymbals,
"Praise Him with resounding cymbals,
"Let everything that has breath praise the Lord.
"Praise the Lord."

~ *Psalm 150:3-6, Student Bible, NIV*

Though I enjoyed dancing growing up, I never took formal dance lessons or found that that was one activity I just could not live without. So when I felt myself being called to this ministry, I was somewhat perplexed about why I was drawn so strongly to this form of communicating. A few years ago, during a Spiritual Gifts class at my church, one of the teachers, Beverly Coleman, offered a lot of clarification. She said something like, *"Your gift is not dance, your gift is exhortation, which you use in dance."* That made perfect sense to me, as I know one of my spiritual gifts is *exhortation* (encouragement) (Romans 12:6, 8).

That means that God may use dance as the vehicle through which your spiritual gift --- teaching, pastoring, healing or evangelism, for instance --- is exercised. To learn more about how spiritual gifts are used in arts ministry, check out Rev. Stephanie Butler Adams' book *"My Body Is The Temple: Encounters and Revelations of Sacred Dance and Artistry"* (2002, Xulon Press). In a chapter in this book, she discusses how spiritual gifts should be used in worship-arts ministry, to make the best impact *for* God's Kingdom.

"Work It Out!"

~ Chapter 3 ~

Now that you're spiritually suited up, let's move to the physical. I'm not sure what shape you're entering the ministry in, but I am probably at my most physically fit – over my entire life! --- now that I am praise dancing. Because of the physical requirements of my ministry, my endurance level has increased, as there have been many Sunday morning worship services that I ministered for at least 30 minutes at a time! Just this past Resurrection Sunday, my dance ministry was asked to minster for our 7:45 a.m. worship service, and then we turned right around to minister at our regularly scheduled 11:00 a.m. worship service! That, we all felt!

But I didn't start there, able to minister through dance constantly for 30 minutes at a time; and if that's where you find yourself, don't worry, you will also move to a level of healthy endurance. Make sure, though, that before you start ministering, you have the go-ahead from your physician.

You will and can train your body to perform certain dance moves. For instance, the dance ministry I first started ministering with was fond of fan kicks (a lift of the leg as it follows the shape of an arc --- like a folding hand fan --- moving from one corner to another). Sadly, my fan kicks looked more like 'ground' kicks, as they were mere inches off the floor. I was very frustrated that my legs could move no higher than they did: Was something wrong with my body? The answer was 'no,' not at all; my leg and hip muscles were just not that flexible. So over time, I worked on my fan kicks --- sometimes standing in front of my bedroom mirror, anywhere in the house, maybe even out in the supermarket, wherever the unction hit me. Now, I hear some newer dancers to the ministry saying the same thing I used to say. There's nothing wrong with your body or theirs, other than that it's out of shape. Also, remember that the exercises and moves you make on one side of your body, need to be done on the other side, so that one side of your body does not grow stronger than the other side does.

Then, there was another time I started experiencing stiffness in my left hip area. Before I could make an appointment to get it checked out, I went to a dance conference, where a woman with a beautiful spirit led the class through a morning stretch that was nothing sort of a true "morning glory" experience with the Lord! I pressed through her body-work exercises, knowing that my poor little hip area was not in the best shape. It seemed that within an hour of doing those gentle stretches, however, that annoying little pain was gone.

> *Put on your favorite gospel CD or Playlist and stretch and dance as you meet God for a "Morning Glory" session!*

That's been more than two years ago! So, what am I saying? **Work it out!**

Start a safe, daily exercise and stretching program, starting slowly first and building up your routine and stamina. *(You can create your own "morning glory" routine, where you meet with the Lord, to stretch out and dance before Him! Put on your favorite playlist of gospel songs or your best music CD!)* Exercise programs like Zumba® or Bokwa® (though this not an endorsement for or against these programs) offer fun, high-energy and weight-reducing ways to move to your personal best!

Learn from a professional dance teacher or a certified fitness expert about how to properly work out, so that your knees, ankles, wrists, arms, back, neck and other body parts are safely stretched and able to do the work of the ministry!

Then, just *"work it out!"*

"Consecrate in the Shadows"

~ Chapter 4 ~

Early on in my "public" praise-dance ministry, there was a time when I would practice my dance choreographies at night, often with just the light from an outdoor street lamp illuminating the inside of my living room. Those seemed to be the times that I moved from the choreographed into the *'spontaneous'* or my sheer worship of God --- being manifested through my dance. It was just a "me and Him" time, my intimate space before The Lord, an emptying out of me, a pouring in of Him . . . *It was God 'consecrating me' in the shadows.*

    Consecration means *"dedicated to a sacred purpose,"* according to Merriam Webster online.

    Then, when I ministered in public, it was easier to share with folks what I felt God was saying through a song or lyrics or what I felt He was calling me to communicate at that time; I was sharing out of that consecration, that secret time with God, out of that *'dedication of that dance for His purpose.'*

> *"But when you pray, go into your room,*
> *close the door and pray to your Father, who is unseen.*
> *Then your Father, who sees what is done in secret,*
> *will reward you."*
> ~ Matthew 6:6 (NIV)

That *'consecrated time with* God' is like my prayer time and that time spent with God is something that I believe many onlookers can sense and feel when they experience dance-ministers in worship. We should want to, and need to, spend time being "in the presence of God" if we desire His Glory to show forth on the countenance of our dance, just as the people saw the radiance on Moses' face when he descended from Mount Sinai (Exodus 34:29). We should want and need Him to go forth with us in our dance, to show up at some point while we are ministering!

Now, go ahead and consecrate in the shadows, so you can dance with His glory into the marvelous light!

"Just Flow . . ."

~ Chapter 5 ~

I'm reminded of a time when my church's youth dance ministry joined the adults for a previously unrehearsed morning worship service. Because the youth were not as trained as the adults were in 'flowing" without choreography ---dancing without the benefit of rehearsed dance steps and moves --- they were at a loss about what to do or how to dance and move . . . and it looked like they felt out of place.

In part, because they probably did not practice what I mentioned in the past chapter --- the "consecration in the shadows' --- they were unsure or uncomfortable with "just flowing" with whatever the Holy Spirit directed them to do. (A few years later, though, some in this same youth dance ministry ministered with the adults again in unscripted praise and worship, and they ministered so awesomely!)

The more time you spend "consecrating in the shadows," the more you will feel comfortable flowing in the light when the worship is impromptu or unscripted (meaning, there is no choreography, no previously rehearsed dance steps). When I first started praise dancing, I often reminded myself to *"dance like no one was watching"* --- the same way I danced in the shadows in my living room.

Or, when you're dancing, just remind yourself that you are dancing *for* and *before* The Lord.

What would that look like? Got a picture? Great, now Just flow!

What do you know about 'commanding your space'? *Keep reading!*

Commanding your space . . .

- Dance **BIG !!!** *(that's 'big'!)*
- Emote with your face.
- Show forth your passion!
- Use your space --- don't be timid in your movements!
- Move your feet ~ cover territory!

POWER POINTS

- *Put on some gospel or Christian music and dance, without inhibition in your bedroom or living room!*

- *Imagine that you are dancing before God's throne: How would you dance? What would you do?*

- *Create a one to two-minute dance that you would want to teach to someone else.*

"Just One More Time"

~ Chapter 6 ~

More than I'm proud to admit, there have been times when my dance ministry has presented a dance, and, after review, I note that if *I* had done just one or two more full-out practices, my part in the dance could have been more fluid or more powerful. Or, there were times when my dance ministry did a specially choreographed dance a second or third time . . . *and we could all see that that dance only got better and more fluid each time it was presented!*

Practice really does make *perfect-ed!* Respect the *'drill sergeant' in your ministry,* that person whose job it is to make you run through the dance just one more time! *(Shout out to all the Candice Marshalls, aka your drill sergeant, in ministry!)* Come ministry time, *you will probably be very happy that you acquiesced to their direction!* So, don't hate --- imitate!

Then, at home, practice on the dance again --- get that 'dance' and the message of the dance in your spirit. Figure out how you learn, what your dance learning style is and move with that method.

At the onset of my public praise-dance ministry, just looking at someone perform a move in front of me was about 50 percent effective *(really, less than that!).* I had to write out the moves, making my special notations and drawings on the right half and margins of my song lyrics sheet. Over the years, though, my learning style has changed. I can, now, see someone do a move and learn from that. I still, though, use the note-taking and picture drawing for certain parts of the dance and for those times when I am teaching choreography. I am also known to use sound effects for dance moves or use my own brand of phrasing to remember a move. For instance, in Israel Houghton's song *"I Am A Friend of God's,"* my *"bend down and scoop up the flower bouquet and turn and toss it into the air to God"* looks like a dancer bending down to the right and crossing the arms down low, then rising up, turning upper torso to the left to lift the hands and cross the arms in awe to God . . .

Whatever it takes . . . Work to give God your best --- that's your very best (Col. 3:23).

"Whatever you do, work at it with all your heart, as working for the Lord, not for men, since you know that you will receive an inheritance from the Lord as your reward. It is the Lord Christ you are serving."
~ Colossians 3:23-24, Student Bible, NIV

'Dance Marking'

Did you know that research says 'dance marking' --- rehearsing a dance in your head, as opposed to physically executing it --- is good for helping to remember the dance and remember it more precisely? This study was organized by Dr. Edward Warburton, a professor of dance at the University of California-Santa Cruz, himself a former professional ballet dancer

~ *Psychological Science* (July 23, 2013)

"Listen To What God Says"

~ Chapter 7 ~

When you start praise dancing and especially when you start developing more of an ear for God, He will begin to talk to you about your ministry and your walk with Him.

He will even start to speak to you about your dance choreography, even if you don't envision yourself as a choreographer. It doesn't matter whether you see yourself being this or not: He is God, and as The Master Dance Teacher, He can do anything He wants to. He is *omnipresent (Everywhere Present), omniscient (All Knowing), omnipotent (All Powerful)!*

Even when you are in the midst of actual ministry, God will speak to you while you are dancing. He might direct you to dance to a particular song or to dance with a certain person or group. He may even direct you to share your streamer or flag with an onlooker.

Be obedient. Make sure you live in such a way that you can hear what God is saying to you *(John 10:27)!* As I'm writing this, I'm reminded to say that it's expected that you are under the spiritual covering of a pastor and church; that you are a faithful member of assembly; and that you are regularly attending worship service (Hebrews 10:25) and Bible study (2 Timothy 2:15) and ministering with your tithe (Malachi 3:10 and Acts 20:35)!

If you have questions about this, take them to God. You may also want to consider sharing with your

Pastor, your Sunday School/Fulfillment Hour or small-group teacher or another trusted leader at your church.

What do you hear God telling you about your personal praise-dance ministry?

_____

_____

_____

_____

Your response: *How and when are you responding?*

_____

_____

_____

_____

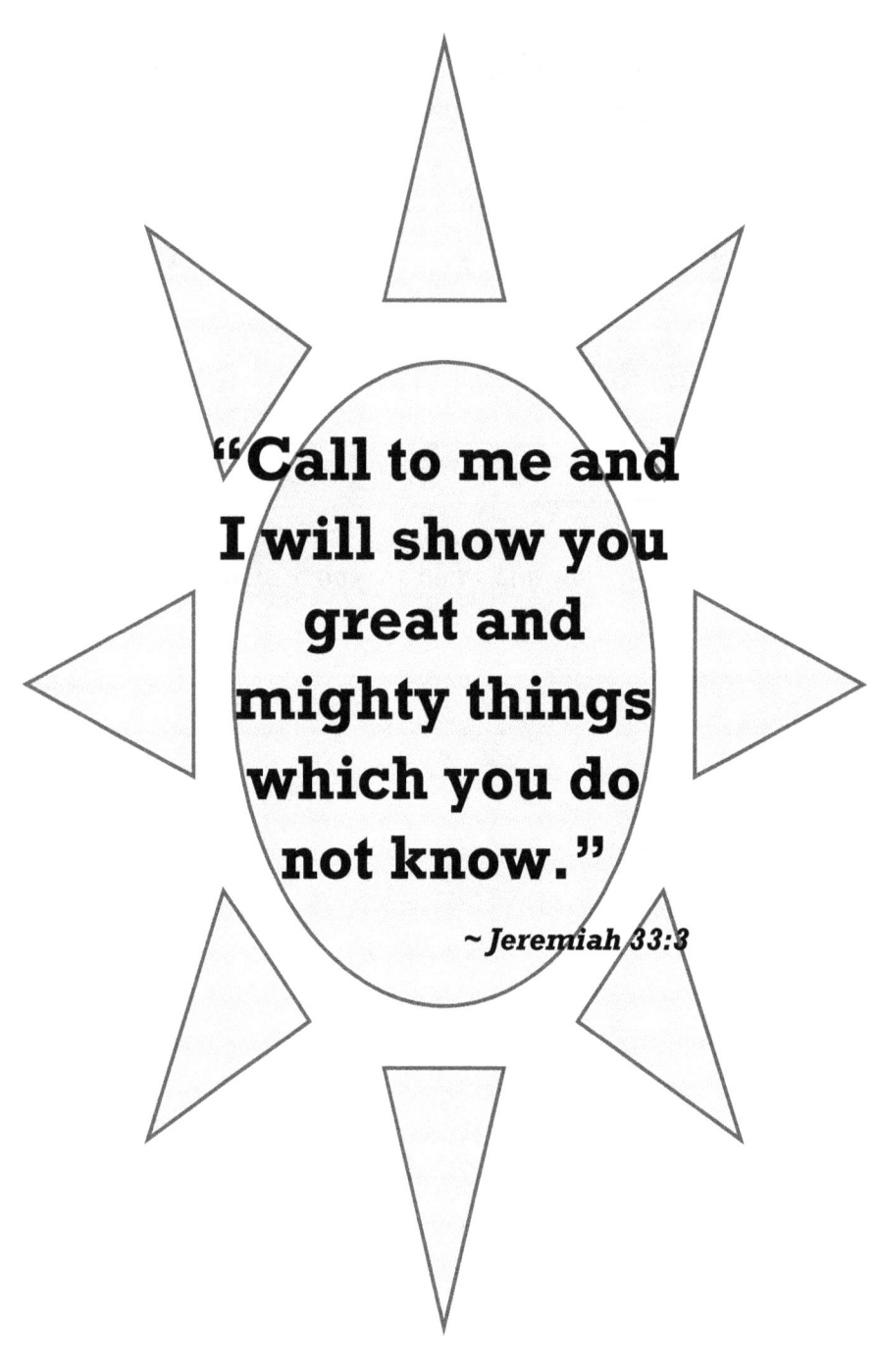

"Call to me and I will show you great and mighty things which you do not know."

~ *Jeremiah 33:3*

"No Grief, Please!"

~ Chapter 8 ~

This particular chapter reminds me of the scripture in the Bible that advises us to not make our leaders' jobs difficult... Hebrews 13:17.

> *"Be responsive to your pastoral leaders. Listen to their counsel. They are alert to the condition of your lives and work under the strict supervision of God. Contribute to the joy of their leadership, not its drudgery. Why would you want to make things harder for them?"*
> ~ Hebrews 13:17 (The Message version)

Yes, why would we want to make ministry work harder for our ministry leaders, who are an extension of our pastoral leaders?

I'm reminded of the night that our dance leader, Cheryl Wright, had a sort of 'coming-to-Jesus' talk about our promptness. Did we need to move the time back, she asked. No, because a few of us were running off after practice to pick up children from work or get younger ones into bed at a decent time for school the next day. Then, she shared that she often skipped an early dinner, as she was running to make sure she got to practice before us... only to rush there and be still sitting there, alone, minutes after our practice should have started.

So we endeavored to get better... This point is to remind us to especially respect the time of others, especially our leaders.

Let's endeavor to arrive to practice on time, if not _ahead_ of start time. (What a novel concept, yes?) If we know we're going to be late, send a text message or make a quick telephone call, being sure to leave a voicemail message.

How else can you help your ministry move along further into its mission?

Can you tell them about workshops or other events in which they might want to participate or could learn some techniques to help improve the ministry?

If there is a community wardrobe, what is the system for cleaning it? Could you volunteer and wash the laundry one time (or more!) or help create a system for doing it?

On the wardrobe issue again: 'A stitch in times saves nine.' If there are rips or tears in clothing and you can sew, can you patch up the damage before it becomes larger? If you see that faulty zipper about to destroy a $25 leotard, can you buy a $4 replacement zipper and summon the time and patience to repair that garment?

Honor the practice time: When you come to practice, commit to being 'fully there,' physically and emotionally. Meaning, warm up on time, be present for devotion and give your full attention to your allotted practice time. Don't leave the session to make phone calls, conduct other business or talk to people who 'happen' across the practice session. Follow up with all of that later. Even if you know the routine or have a special part, practice with the group to produce a "synergy" --- a type of energy created from everybody working together to support the common good --- that will translate into beautiful, powerful ministry!

"Pull Your Clothes Together"

~ Chapter 9 ~

As a dance minister, consider strengthening your ministry by building your dance wardrobe. Your wardrobe is what some in the ministry call garments, commonly known as praise-dance clothes. This wardrobe is _yours_ --- not your church's, not your dance ministry's, not your friend's, not your mother's. When you have your own praise-dance wardrobe and you are called or want to dance outside of your organized ministry, you can go forth in excellence without being encumbered with calling friends and others to borrow their garments and hoping they have what you want!

(You should know that the Bible does not say we are required to dress in any way to praise Him; God is always concerned about the 'fashion' or state of our heart.)

When we read Exodus chapters 28 and 39, we learn a lot about how much care the Lord commanded be given to the garments designed for Aaron and his sons. (Some Bibles actually subtitle Exodus 28 as "The Priestly Garments" and has special sections on 'the ephod,' 'the breastpiece' and 'other priestly garments,' such as the turban, tunic, sash and undergarments.) This family of Levites acted as priests, ministering in the temple to God. Exodus 28:2 says these garments were to be made for Aaron *"for glory and for beauty"* to minister before The Lord. What do you think of that standard as it applies to today's ministers of dance?

What would our garments look like if they were *"to symbolize glory and beauty"* (Exodus 28:2, The Message)?

To understand why emphasis is placed on garments, consider this: Suppose you know that each week you want to go to the movies or a football or basketball game or out for dinner. But each week, you call a friend and ask them for something to wear from their closet. *Sounds a bit silly and really inappropriate on some level, doesn't it?* That's how it is with dance garments. If you know you might be called or if you desire to be called for special ministry, then start working now to build your own, personal praise-dance wardrobe!

You should always have your own leotard to minister in --- that garment is a particularly intimate one for you . . . it's *kinda* like your underwear, right? That's not an item you want to borrow --- or loan. Although I know there are occasions when that happens, again, make sure that you don't make that habitual. If you are the one without a leotard, what steps do you need to take <u>now</u> to ensure that you have that garment for your next ministry engagement?

If you loaned that item, do you have an extra leotard that you could just donate to that particular person, or are you in a position to just buy them one?

Grow your dance ministry wardrobe by:

- Starting with basic items, such as leotards, Palazzo pants and skirts, in neutral colors like white and black

- Pay attention to your undergarments, including supportive bras, sports bras and girdles and socks or stockings to match your shoe color. *(Supportive undergarments 'batten down the hatches,' as I like to say, securing body parts to keep them from jiggling, bouncing or otherwise moving and causing distractions during practice <u>and</u> ministry! Again, dance ministers, we do not want to be a stumbling block' to anyone! 'Batten down the hatches!')*

- Don't forget your dance shoes!

- Learn to use large scarves to create attractive drapes as a covering over your leotard.

- Create a budget and a plan for building your wardrobe: What can you sacrifice over the next few months to afford a new garment?

- Is there someone who'd like to swap garments with you?

- Can you sew? Pull out that trusted Singer, Brother or Kenmore sewing machine and consider making your own garments!

- Don't know how to sew? Take a class to learn how and get busy sewing your own garments!

~ Sample Garment Inventory ~

GARMENT (Style Number)	ORIGIN (Acquired from)	SIZE & COLOR	PURCHASE PRICE
LEOTARDS			
PALAZZO PANTS			
DRESSES			
SKIRTS			
OVERLAYS			
SHOES / SANDALS			
UNDERGARMENTS			

"Self-Critique, Please"

~ Chapter 10 ~

As you start ministering in dance, you might want to know how effective you are and how much you have grown. So check in with yourself: Ask, *'self, am I closer to God this year than I was last year? Last month? Have I learned something new for my ministry in the past year? Do I desire to?'*

Unless you have a ministry leader who guides you in this sort of annual or biennial reflection, consider making this a regular practice. This keeps you sharp for your ministry, keeps you and your moves from becoming boring to onlookers and keeps your message pertinent! *There is still so much to learn beyond what you read in this handbook!*

Here are some things to consider:

- Are you growing as a dance minister?
- If so, state three ways you are growing as a dance minister.
- If you aren't growing, why do you think you aren't?
- What new things have you learned in the past year? What new things would you love to learn this year?
- What do you see when you review videotape of your ministry dances?
- What is God telling you about your ministry *(go back to chapter #7, "Listen to What God Says.")*

~ NOTES ~

"Know That You Are and Have a Gift"

~ Chapter 11 ~

The Bible compares the members of a church to parts of the body, noting that each member has a set function. So it is with the dance ministry --- each member brings a special added gift that is manifest through the dance ministry.

Come to know what your particular gifts are: Are you the member who is always concerned about the garments? Are you the one with a particular passion for evangelism and 'outside' events, those where you have the opportunity to tell people about God? Maybe you're the one who is always making sure to keep the toiletries box replenished. Or, maybe your quirkiness manifests itself in bold ideas for choreography or the use of space at your church. Yet, you might be the one more concerned that all members are all kept informed, regularly receiving and reading their messages, whether via telephone, cell phone text, email or Facebook or some other social media outlet.

This chapter is just to affirm that you are OK, that though you might be considered the dancer with a particular 'quirk,' that's just your special gifting that you bring to the ministry. Also know that it really is OK if your fellow dance ministers do not feel as passionately as you do about these particular aspects of the ministry. But just move as God directs you, or as my pastor, Dr.

Rev. Addis Moore of Mt Zion Baptist Church, likes to say, continue operating "*in your set place.*"

> *"But in fact God has arranged the parts in the body, every one of them, just as he wanted them to be . . . "*
> ~ 1 Corinthians 12:18 (NIV)

What are the special gifts you bring to the ministry?

_____

_____

_____

_____

How do these gifts enhance your ministry to grow God's Kingdom?

_____

_____

_____

_____

"Now What?"

~ Chapter 12 ~

One of my favorite YouTube praise-dance videos shows a group of young women dancing to a gospel song on the floor of a basketball court! *How awesome!* I have no idea if it was a <u>*liturgical*</u> dance group or a non-religious dance group that just chose to dance to a gospel song, but I thought "how wonderful!" What a wonderful opportunity --- using a full arena like a basketball court to deliver God's message to the masses!

So often, you will find yourself ministering in the church, before mostly "saved" people or those most likely to accept Christ. Where is the harvest? Most of the harvest is "outside the walls of the church," on a basketball court, at a local park. Consider what I call "taking it to the streets" --- evangelism, or spreading the news about God to others --- at street or block fairs, ball games, juvenile homes or nursing homes, malls or other shopping centers . . . even a public library. Once when I was leaving a

What's evangelism?

The winning or revival of personal commitments to Christ.

(www.merriam-webster.com)

community-housing office, I saw a posted flier about a dance class. I turned around to read the flier, learning that a local woman was offering free dance classes at a branch of the local library! *The library! Our opportunities and places to minister are endless!*

Use your dance ministry to actually minister and evangelize to a world that needs to hear the gospel message --- *that Jesus loves them and is waiting on them!*

Remember the Great Commission: Matthew 28: 19-20.

"Therefore go and make disciples of all nations, baptizing them in the name of the Father and of the Son and of the Holy Spirit, and teaching them to obey everything I have commanded you. And surely I am with you always, to the very end of the age."

~ Matthew 28:19-20 (NIV)

"For God so loved the world that he gave his one and only Son, that whoever believes in him shall not perish but have eternal life."

~ John 3:16 (NIV)

To encourage you to start thinking about taking your ministry 'to the streets,' use the following grid to indicate possible places for you to minister, outside of your church, in the next year.

"Taking It to the Streets"

MONTH	SITE & CONTACT	MINISTRY DATE

~ NOTES ~

PRAISE-DANCE RESOURCES

Christian Dance Fellowship USA *(part of ICDF)*
- http://www.cdfusa.org/

Dancing Preachers International
- www.dancingpreachers.com

Eagles International Training Institute
- www.eaglesiti.org/

His Hem Ministry praise-dance blog *(see next page)*
- www.HisHemMinistry.com

International Christian Dance Fellowship
- http://www.icdf.com/

International Dance Commission
- http://intldancecommission.ning.com/

International Liturgical Dance Fellowship
- http://www.ildf.org

National Liturgical Dance Network
International Liturgical Dance Network
- http://www.natldancenetwork.com

Praise Dance news
- His Hem Ministry praise-dance blog,
    www.HisHemMinistry.com

HIS HEM MINISTRY praise dance

Since June 2009, *His Hem Ministry* has served the praise-dance and worship-arts community by sharing:

- How to use praise dance to grow God's Kingdom
- News about the global dance ministry community
- Information on upcoming conferences, workshops, retreats and other events
- Techniques and strategies for improving one's ministry
- Information on Anointed Garment designers and ways to inexpensively build your dance wardrobe
- Videos from other ministries that highlight that work and encourage viewers
- Biblical teaching about praise dance

For more information, contact **His Hem Ministry** via email at *hishempraise@gmail.com*.

More Books from This Author from Purposed Publishing 8:18

"31 Tips to Enhancing Your Personal Praise Dance Ministry" *by Stephanie Esters*

"And A Child Shall Lead Them"
A Practical and Spiritual Guide to Managing a Youth Praise Dance, Mime or Worship Arts Ministry" by Stephanie Esters

~ *Bibliography* ~

Adams, Rev. Stephanie Butler. *My Body Is The Temple.* Xulon Press, 2002.

"Going Through the Motions Improves Dance Performance." *Psychological Science*: Association for Psychological Science, July 23, 2013. Web. 6 April 2015 Accessed.

~ Reader Reaction ~

We would love to know what you think of this guide: Was it helpful, how could the work be more helpful? Your responses could be included in any future updates to "Omg ~ I'm Praise Dancing! Now What?"

Please direct comments and questions to: Purposed Publishing 8:18 (email HisHemPraise@gmail.com):

_____

_____

_____

_____

_____ .

~ *Index* ~

Aaron 19
Bokwa® 7
Choreography 10, 14, 25
Consecration 8-10
Dance Marking 13
Evangelism .... vi, 25, 27
Evangelism scheduler..................... 29
Flow 10-11
Garments .... vi, 19-20, 25
His Hem Ministry praise dance 31-32
Impromptu dance 10
Listening to God 14-15
Moore, Pastor Dr. Rev. Addis 25
Moses 9
Physical fitness 5-7
Practice 12
Resources 28
Self-assessment (self-evaluation) 23
'Set place' 25
Sewing 18, 21
Sewing machine 21
Spontaneous dance 11
Synergy 18
Zumba® 7

www.ingramcontent.com/pod-product-compliance
Lightning Source LLC
Chambersburg PA
CBHW051712090426
42736CB00013B/2674